LONELINESS
How to Be Alone but Not Lonely

JUNE HUNT

HENDRICKSON PUBLISHERS · ROSE PUBLISHING

CONTENTS

*D*ear Friend,

Have you ever thought about what God was referring to the first time He said the words *"not good"*? Was it going without food or shelter? Was it being selfish or proud? *No.*

In Genesis 2:18 the Lord God said, *"It is not good for the man to be alone."*

God did not design us to be alone. Although there will be periods when we are alone, that is not to be a permanent state. He knows that after a period of time we certainly can become lonely.

Looking back on my life, I remember a time that was painfully poignant. I was stunned by what had happened to a very special relationship. I was so hurt, so deeply wounded, my heart ached with pain.

While I had the support of a loving mother and several true friends, I didn't want to share with them the depth of my pain. Although they knew some details, I didn't feel like I could unload my overwhelming pain onto anyone. And truthfully, nothing that anyone said or did could have lifted the hurt from my heart.

During this time, I went inside a card store, saw a sentiment about tender relationships and suddenly my eyes filled with tears. And, I remember having tears all the way through a movie about a loving relationship. (As a "non-crier," that was very unusual.) I could hardly believe my response. However, the loss of a relationship—whether by death, divorce, or rejection of any kind—can leave us feeling devastated.

We can feel so lonely, so separated, so isolated, thinking no one really understands. Yet God understands our deepest times of loneliness. He knows the heaviness of our hurt.

Jesus said, *"Take my yoke upon you"* (Matthew 11:29). He is willing, and even *wants,* to lighten the burden of your heavy heart. Then, in turn, He will use your sensitive heart to be a source of strength to help others.

In time, you can be God's instrument of compassion to come alongside and lighten the hearts of those who are lonely.

What I've personally learned is this: When my heart has been pressed down with pain, that is when my relationship with the Lord has grown deeper ... deeper ... deeper.

In times of loneliness and sorrow, take this verse to heart ...

"I cry to you, O LORD; I say, 'You are my refuge, my portion in the land of the living.'"
(Psalm 142:5)

Yours in the Lord's hope,

June

June Hunt

LONELINESS
How to Be Alone but Not Lonely

Have you ever wondered: When is the first time God says, *"It is not good?"* Is it when Adam and Eve eat the forbidden fruit? Is it when they hide from God? Is it when they refuse to take responsibility for their disobedience?

Actually, prior to all these events, God states in no uncertain terms:

"It is not good for the man to be alone."
(Genesis 2:18)

God Himself speaks these words after creating the first human being—the crowning glory of His creation, made in God's image. Adam is surrounded by indescribable beauty in the Garden of Eden with its unlimited fruit, lush foliage, and a wide array of wildlife. Yet, there is something missing—rather, *someone*.

God causes a deep sleep to come over Adam and removes one of his ribs to form a woman. Then God presents her to Adam, and he is no longer *alone*.

If you are cut off from relationships, living in isolation, coping alone day by day, God considers this *"not good."* While the Lord doesn't lead everyone to marry, He does call everyone to be involved with people. *People,* not just charming pets, not just prized possessions, but *people.* You are called to show interest in people, to express care to people, to sacrificially love people. Remember, Adam was surrounded by animals and objects of beauty in the Garden, yet God considered him "alone." And that is why ...

**"The Lord God said ...
'I will make a helper suitable for him.'"
(Genesis 2:18)**

▶ **Chronic loneliness** often leads to personal isolation, bitterness, and destructive behavior.

- Can result in having "no hope of connecting again in the future"[7]

- Can end in "suicide or angry, violent alienation"[8]

"When my heart was grieved and my spirit embittered, I was senseless and ignorant; I was a brute beast before you." (Psalm 73:21–22)

Active Yet Lonely

QUESTION: "My life is active and full, so why do I get lonely?"

ANSWER: Activity alone is not a cure for loneliness. Over-involvement in activities—to the point where you have no solitude—can be an attempt to numb the longing in your heart for God.

"Find rest, O my soul, in God alone;
my hope comes from him.
He alone is my rock and my salvation;
he is my fortress, I will not be shaken."
(Psalm 62:5–6)

Are you comfortable spending time alone, solitary, and separate from others? Or, do you prefer to spend your waking hours surrounded by people, noise, and activity because you associate quiet, private time with loneliness and emptiness?

Actually, spending time alone—seeking the peace and quiet of solitude—can bring serenity to your spirit.

Solitary time spent in prayer or Bible study can also broaden your perspective and deepen your faith. Psalm 46:10 encourages you to: *"Be still, and know that I am God."* By seeking times of solitude, you put aside your worldly concerns and simply listen for God's voice. Doing so helps you discern His intended path so that you can choose it as your own.

> **"Let the morning bring me word of your unfailing love, for I have put my trust in you. Show me the way I should go, for to you I lift up my soul." (Psalm 143:8)**

▶ **Being alone** means being solitary, "separated from others."[9]

- *Alone* in the New Testament is sometimes translated from the Greek word *monos,* which means "alone, by oneself."[10]

- Jesus often sought solitude. He separated Himself from others in order to commune alone with the Father.

15

"After he had dismissed them, he went up on a mountainside by himself to pray. When evening came, he was there alone." (Matthew 14:23)

▶ **Being alone** can be positive or negative.

- *Alone* in the Old Testament is sometimes translated from the Hebrew word *băd*, which means "alone, by one's self, apart."[11]

- Moses was settling disputes all alone from morning to evening, wearing himself out. He needed the help of others.

"You and these people who come to you will only wear yourselves out. The work is too heavy for you; you cannot handle it alone." (Exodus 18:18)

Wanting Time Alone

QUESTION: **"At times I feel like I must get away by myself, but my mate worries that this is a negative reflection on us. I love and enjoy our relationship. Is there something wrong with me in wanting time alone?"**

ANSWER: No, solitude is time spent physically apart from all others, which can be good for you. Warren Wiersbe observed, "Jesus used to go out by Himself to meditate and to pray. ... The apostle Paul left his friends so he could walk and meditate while they traveled by ship. He wanted solitude. He wanted to be alone."[12]

Solitude is "the quality or state of being alone or remote from society."[13] Most people believe that being alone is the same thing as being lonely. However, they are usually basing their thinking on their own painful experience.

▶ **Healthy solitude is ...**[14]

- A state of being "alone, but not necessarily lonely"[15]

- A chosen separation from the press of people

- A needed refuge from the noise and negativity of life

- A place of privacy "to sort out ideas, values, and attitudes"[16]

- A healthy haven from unhealthy emotions

- A positive time alone without being preoccupied with missing others

- A shelter from the storm to handle significant loss

- A personal retreat to prime the pump of creativity

- A private sanctuary to rest, pray, and meditate

"At daybreak Jesus went out to a solitary place. ... One of those days Jesus went out to a mountainside to pray, and spent the night praying to God." (Luke 4:42; 6:12)

Our language has wisely sensed the two sides of being alone. It has created the word *loneliness* to express the pain of being alone. And it has created the word *solitude* to express the glory of being alone.

—*Paul Tillich, Christian theologian*[17]

Part of the difference between being alone and being lonely involves the sense of being in control.

Solitude is being alone by choice.[18] It is deliberately seeking quiet, private alone time to reflect, to be in prayer, or simply to be still and listen for God's voice. As Psalm 37:7 suggests, *"Be still before the LORD and wait patiently for him."*

Loneliness, on the other hand, is the emotion that arises when you feel that you have little control over being alone.[19] You feel isolated and abandoned, and wish your circumstances were different. Often this is a consequence of a change in your life—a move, a death, a broken relationship, or any situation where you find yourself wishing for attachments you once enjoyed.

"Look to my right and see; no one is concerned for me. I have no refuge; no one cares for my life."
(Psalm 142:4)

Here are other distinctions between being alone and being lonely:[20]

▶ **Being alone** refers to the *physical*—the state of being separated from others.

▶ **Being lonely** refers to the *emotional*—the state of feeling isolated, rejected, or desolate.

▶ **Being alone** can be a *positive experience*—a time of creativity and communion with the Lord.

▶ **Being lonely** is always a *negative feeling,* often accompanied by feelings of hopelessness.

Loneliness Is Usually Temporary

QUESTION: "Does loneliness last forever?"

ANSWER: No. Typically, loneliness is temporary and diminishing as you become more accepting and comfortable with your loss or change in life. And remember, one day, when you are with God, there will be no more loneliness, no more death, no more mourning, no more tears.

"He will wipe every tear from
their eyes. There will be no more death
or mourning or crying or pain,
for the old order of things
has passed away."
(Revelation 21:4)

CHARACTERISTICS OF LONELY PEOPLE

He is chosen of God—he is God's anointed—but David feels desperately alone and lonely. His loneliness wreaks havoc with his body, weakening his bones and sapping his strength. God's choice king likens himself to *"a broken vessel,"* his life in shards with the jagged pieces piercing his emotions, weakening his very soul.

In describing the devastation of his loneliness, David says he is a *"contempt"* to his neighbors, and he is a *"dread"* to his friends (Psalm 31:11).

In a fleeting moment of fear, David even feels like the Lord has abandoned him, but then his faith swells and his hope returns.

He boldly proclaims ...

"Be strong and take heart,
all you who hope in the LORD."
(Psalm 31:24)

As a lonely person, you can get to the place where you "automatically build walls instead of bridges"—you "step back when others step" toward you.[21]

By continuously using language like the statements below, you can actually create your own world of isolation, receiving the exact opposite response than the one you want. These self-defeating "I" statements focus selfishly on self-protection. They are wall building instead of bridge building, keeping you stuck in a state of loneliness.

> "An unfriendly man pursues selfish ends;
> he defies all sound judgment."
> (Proverbs 18:1)

> "My kinsmen have gone away;
> my friends have forgotten me."
> (Job 19:14)

Loneliness Checklist

Check (✓) each of the following statements that apply to you.

☐ "I feel all alone."

☐ "I don't believe anyone understands the way I feel."

☐ "I don't really matter to anyone."

☐ "I don't have any good qualities that draw people to me."

☐ "I don't have anything to offer to a relationship."

☐ "I can't seem to connect with other people."

☐ "I will never find anyone to love me."

☐ "I don't feel like I fit in with anyone."

☐ "I'm tired of trying to make people like me. I always fail."

☐ "I always feel excluded."

☐ "I'm always on the outside."

☐ "I'm too messed up for anyone to like me or want to be around me."

☐ "I'm just a born loser."

☐ "I feel like I've been deserted."

☐ "I don't deserve to be loved or to have friends."

☐ "I think I'm the only one who feels like this."

Feelings of loneliness are easier to describe than to define. Loneliness is a feeling of emptiness in the pit of your stomach when someone you love has deserted you. You feel abandoned, unwanted, or unneeded, as if "you're all by yourself when you're actually surrounded by all kinds of people."[22] You feel like no one really cares.

These problems can intensify if you start to believe your loneliness signals a serious personal defect—that you are somehow unacceptable, unworthy, immature, weak, or unlovable. If this happens, you may begin to feel you have nothing to live for. Your pain can erode your self-esteem, drain your strength, and steal your hope.[23]

Loneliness puts a wall around you no matter how free you actually may be.

If you are lonely, you may identify with this passage from Psalm 31:9–12 in which an emotionally devastated David prays to God.

"Be merciful to me, O LORD, for I am in distress; my eyes grow weak with sorrow, my soul and my body with grief. My life is consumed by anguish and my years by groaning; my strength fails because of my affliction, and my bones grow weak Because of all my enemies, I am the utter contempt of my neighbors; I am a dread to my friends—those who see

me on the street flee from me.
I am forgotten by them as though I were
dead; I have become like broken pottery."
(Psalm 31:9–12)

▶ **Persistent loneliness** can lead to other problems, such as:

- Depression

- Anger

- Fear

- Fault-finding in others

- Self-criticism

▶ **People who are perpetually lonely:**

- Have difficulty taking risks socially, such as introducing themselves to others, starting a conversation, or joining a group

- Feel uncomfortable sharing personal feelings

- Have difficulty trusting others in a social situation

- Develop a pessimistic or cynical outlook on life

- Expect to be rejected by others

▶ **When loneliness becomes severe:**

- Thinking is altered

- Outlook on life changes

- Motivation is lost

- Hopelessness abounds

- Isolation deepens

Loneliness can leave you desperate to connect with *anybody*, leading you to impulsively involve yourself too quickly or too deeply with those who are not "suitable helpers." The result will be the forming of unhealthy, damaging relationships.

> **"A righteous man is cautious
> in friendship, but the way of
> the wicked leads them astray."**
> **(Proverbs 12:26)**

Loneliness can take a toll on your physical health, because what negatively affects your mind and spirit ultimately has a negative impact on your body.

> **"So my spirit grows faint within me; my heart within me is dismayed."**
> **(Psalm 143:4)**

▶ **Physical symptoms of loneliness** are similar to symptoms of stress or depression and may show up as: [24]

- Anxiety and apprehension

- Change in eating habits—loss of appetite or overeating

- Change in sleeping habits—insomnia or oversleeping

- Decreased immunity to illness

- Gastrointestinal problems—stomachaches, nausea, diarrhea

- Headaches

- High blood pressure

- Nervousness

> **"An anxious heart weighs a man down."**
> **(Proverbs 12:25)**

CAUSES FOR LONELINESS

He is the most respected man in all the land, and no one equals him in wealth and wisdom in the eyes of God. When as judge he took his seat in the city square he said, *"the young men saw me and stepped aside and the old men rose to their feet. ... Men listened to me expectantly, waiting in silence for my counsel. ... They waited for me as for showers and drank in my words as the spring rain"* (Job 29:8, 21, 23).

Therefore, there can be no more dramatic descent than what this man—so marveled by others—experiences as when he is found sitting in a pile of ashes, considered a social outcast, and even worse, a sinner. Once revered, Job is now reviled.

Satan has been at work, allowed by God to pummel Job with painful trials and afflictions, including oozing sores from head to toe. All of this occurs not because Job is a "bad man," but because he is blameless before God and his faith is in the spotlight in a supernatural showdown between God and Satan. *Will Job curse God once His hedge of protection is removed?* That is the piercing proposition Satan puts before God! And it is the question asked about you when loneliness invades your life, knocking you to your knees.

Loneliness. Even the word sounds painful, bringing up unhappy memories from the past. Were you the one teased about your looks in childhood or the shy, quiet one everyone overlooked? Maybe your best friend moved to a different city or your dad moved out of the house when you were young.

Everyone struggles with feelings of loneliness, for no one escapes separation, loss, grief, isolation, and the human need for relationships. You were created to live in partnership with others and with God. "The story of Adam and Eve indicates they were partners in relationship to each other, to creation, and to their Creator. ... In life and in death, we long for human community."[25]

As Paul wrote ...

> **"For none of us lives to himself alone and none of us dies to himself alone."**
> **(Romans 14:7)**

Job seemingly has lost it all—his property and livestock, children, health, and friends, except for a trio who further traumatize poor Job with misguided and even malicious counsel.

Job languishes in loneliness, longing for the relationships that once so richly blessed his life. *"He has alienated my brothers from me; my acquaintances are completely estranged from me. My kinsmen have gone away; my friends have forgotten me. My guests and my maidservants count me a stranger; they look upon me as an alien. ... I am loathsome to my own brothers"* (Job 19:13–15, 17).

> **"All my intimate friends detest me; those I love have turned against me."**
> **(Job 19:19)**

The one constant in life is change. We all know this to be true. And yet when change happens to us—especially without warning—we often have difficulty adapting. When your world changes and you are no longer able to predict what will happen next, you can lose confidence and feel uncertain, which often leads to fear. This is the perfect "emotional climate" for loneliness to take root.

Loneliness is an emotion that can strike anyone, young or old, outgoing or introverted, confident or uncertain. Because you have been created to have a relationship with God and with others, you become especially vulnerable to loneliness when you experience rejection or another significant loss. No one escapes feelings of loneliness.

It may help you to remember that God allows these feelings to enter our lives so that we may turn our hearts toward Him for comfort and assurance and toward others who are also lonely.

> "My ears had heard of you
> but now my eyes have seen you."
> (Job 42:5)

Feelings of loneliness are often associated with:

▶ **Circumstances**

Singleness, divorce, death of a loved one, empty nest, loss of a job or home, demotion at work, major move

▶ **Holidays**

Unfulfilled expectations, separation from family or friends, loss of traditional celebrations, memories of the past, lack of plans

▶ **Affliction**

Physical disability, mental or emotional disability, chronic or terminal illness, aging, abuse

▶ Naivety

Taking on responsibilities previously performed by another person, lack of experience in new areas of decision making, disloyal family members

▶ Goals

New career or career change, retirement, job advancement, pursuit of higher education

▶ Estrangement

Absence of intimacy, rejection by others, adulterous spouse, removal from customary environment, marital separation, living or working in new surroundings, rebellious adult children, conflict with friends or fellow employees

When you turn to God in times of loneliness, taking comfort from His steadfast presence and abiding love, your life can be doubly blessed. You can experience God's peace yourself, which empowers you to reach out to other hurting hearts. In this way, you become a living expression of God's concern for all who experience trouble of any sort.

"Praise be to the God and Father of our Lord Jesus Christ, the Father of compassion and the God of all comfort, who comforts us in all our troubles, so that we can comfort those in any trouble with the comfort we ourselves have received from God."
(2 Corinthians 1:3–4)

QUESTION: "When is loneliness most likely to occur?"

ANSWER: Loneliness is felt most often when a major change in life occurs. Most of us struggle with the realities of change even when the change is ultimately for the best. Most of us resist losing both the comforting support of loved ones and the security of the old and familiar. Grief surrounding a significant loss is fertile ground for loneliness to take root and grow.

"My God, my God,
why have you forsaken me?
Why are you so far from saving me,
so far from the words of my groaning?"
(Psalm 22:1)

Fully aware of God's sovereignty in his suffering, Job proclaims, *"the hand of God has struck me"* (Job 19:21).

And yet oblivious to the fiery test of faith he is undergoing, Job believes he is being dealt with unjustly and vows he will maintain his integrity to the very end. Job accuses God of stripping him of his honor, blocking his way, and shrouding his paths in darkness. *"He tears me down on every side till I am gone; he uproots my hope like a tree"* (Job 19:10).

And to one of his cantankerous counselors who ignorantly accuses Job of sinning and calls for his repentance, Job proclaims, *"then know that God has wronged me and drawn his net around me"* (Job 19:6).

When bad things happen to you and when it seems as if your whole world has changed overnight, you feel overwhelmed and "disconnected." Nothing makes sense, and in your frustration and pain, you may blame God or feel unworthy of His love. You may ask yourself, *If God loves me, why would He allow me to suffer?*

Times like these test your faith greatly as you are called to keep on believing in a loving, wise God, who understands your suffering and carries you through dark times. The truth is, it is not for you to figure out why you, or anyone, must endure suffering. That knowledge is God's alone. In the meantime, take hope from His own promise.

> "'For I know the plans I have for you,'
> declares the LORD,
> 'plans to prosper you and not to harm you,
> plans to give you hope and a future.'"
> (Jeremiah 29:11)

Couples often feel spiritually estranged from one another when having marital problems. It is difficult to pray with your mate and experience spiritual oneness if there is discord between you.

▶ **Prayer can be the one thing that can replace:**[26]

- *Misunderstanding* with clarity

- *Defensiveness* with security

- *Blaming* with acceptance

- *Self-interest* with mutual interest

- *Power struggles* with partnership

- *Isolation* with intimacy

- *Anger* with patience

- *Dissention* with peace

> "Devote yourselves to prayer,
> being watchful and thankful."
> (Colossians 4:2)

Estranged from God

QUESTION: "Why does God seem so distant when I'm lonely?"

ANSWER: It is natural to feel deep loneliness when you experience a difficult change or painful loss in your life. But if you indulge in self-pity and become angry at God for your circumstances, you will begin to feel estranged from Him and will fail to receive His loving comfort. You will also set yourself up to SIN by ...

SELF-PITY

Failure to accept responsibility for staying in the rut of your own negative thinking

INDEPENDENCE

Seeking to escape the pain of loneliness in your own way instead of seeking God

NEGLECT

Failure to cultivate your relationship with God and others

**"Come near to God
and he will come near to you."
(James 4:8)**

All people feel lonely at times, but the differences between men and women cause us to experience loneliness in different ways and for different reasons. Unmarried individuals and married couples whose relationships are crippled by loneliness are caught in the current cultural whirlwind of changing roles and misplaced expectations.

Relationship rules have changed. Men and women are floundering with no solid, biblical foundation on which to build a stable, secure relationship. They're unable to build a bridge to one another that can withstand the pressures of a changing society.

What worked for our parents and grandparents does not easily work for couples in today's culture. Many societal supports necessary for forming close family relationships, for building strong emotional bridges, have been discarded. Couples are finding it next to impossible to build something on nothing. Those who try often end up emotionally battered and bruised.

Having an understanding of the components leading to loneliness within these relationships can be helpful in trying to follow God's blueprint for building emotional bridges between marriage partners.

In Genesis we learn that ...

"The man said, 'This is now bone of my bones and flesh of my flesh; she shall be called "woman," for she was taken out of man.' For this reason a man will leave his father and mother and be united to his wife, and they will become one flesh." (Genesis 2:23–24)

When God's blueprint is not followed ...

▶ **A woman typically ...** [27]

- Marries or lives with a boyfriend during her early to mid-twenties and begins feeling lonely in her late twenties

- Becomes frustrated and agitated with her mate in her early to mid-thirties and is depressed in her forties

- Considers her mate unable or unwilling to give her emotional support

- Feels left out of her mate's life and isolated from him even when in the same room together

- Blames her mate for her loneliness

- Seeks counseling for depression and/or anxiety

- Feels isolated and somewhat estranged from other people, even close friends

- Believes her loneliness will end if her mate was out of her life

- Fantasizes about her mate dying and/or leaving her

- Thinks no one really knows or understands her

- Struggles with emotional exhaustion

- Seeks to get her emotional relationship needs met through her children or friends

**"The wise woman builds her house,
but with her own hands
the foolish one tears hers down."
(Proverbs 14:1)**

▶ **A man typically ...** [28]

- Has less relational skills than his wife or live-in girlfriend

- Expresses emotions, empathy, and compassion far less than his female counterpart

- Develops few close friendships and feels no real need for them

- Competes excessively with other men to easily form close emotional relationships with them

- Experiences more isolation but less loneliness than his mate

- Has an aversion to displaying emotions because of societal taboos

- Lacks deep relationships due to his reluctance to express his feelings

- Resists the idea of fellowshipping with other men just for the sake of enjoying one another's company

- Gets together with friends for fun and games, but not for in-depth sharing

- Has no male role model to show him how to drop his "macho mask" and get in touch with his feelings

- Strives for self-sufficiency and seeks to solve problems on his own without being a burden to others

- Prioritizes professional success (from which he derives his identity) over relational success

"A kind man benefits himself, but a cruel man brings trouble on himself."
(Proverbs 11:17)

Lonely Couples

QUESTION: "Why are couples becoming increasingly lonely?"

ANSWER: Living with someone—married or not—does not insure emotional intimacy or security in the relationship. Many couples are not emotionally connected because they do not share their dreams or desires, their trials or temptations, their hurts or hopes. They fail to listen to one another and merely share the roof over their heads.

Therefore, many couples experience "together loneliness"—being physically together but emotionally estranged and isolated, not feeling understood or appreciated. Instead of feeling wanted inside the warm security of home life, they feel an *unwelcome coldness* or an *apathetic indifference* inside their sterile, stymied existence.

> "I lie awake; I have become
> like a bird alone on a roof."
> (Psalm 102:7)

WHY DO People Seem to Be Experiencing More and More Loneliness?

There are several reasons loneliness is on the increase.[29]

▶ **People are becoming more urban** and less rural.

- The closer people live to one another, the more they tend to emotionally isolate from one another.

- The further people live from one another, the more they tend to emotionally become closer.

- Rural communities have a much greater sense of community than urban communities.

▶ **People are much more transient** than in years past.

- Those who move on a regular basis are reluctant to "put down roots" anywhere.

- People who move often "know" more people but don't know how to "get to know" people in an intimate way.

- Frequent movers isolate from others, feeling it is emotionally too painful to get close to people and then have to move away from them.

▶ **People place a high value on mobility**, privacy, and convenience.

- Many people spend their spare time traveling rather than staying home and spending time with their neighbors and friends.

- The desire for privacy drives many people to fence themselves in and others out.

- Since establishing relationships takes time and energy—which is often inconvenient—many decide it is not worth the trouble.

▶ **People are no longer maintaining** intact families.

- The increased divorce rate fragments families and damages or destroys primary relationships.

- Separation of elderly family members from younger members leads to isolation and a crisis in relationship between generations.

- Parents having different work schedules become estranged from one another and sometimes from their children.

▶ **People are becoming less and less involved** in neighborhood churches.

- Many churchgoers see and interact with each other only for a limited amount of time when attending weekly church services.

- Church "socials" in urban areas are often centered around eating and making light conversation rather than on meeting one another's emotional needs.

- Lack of Christian community leads many members to establish superficial relationships rather than deep, Christ-centered friendships.

**"I am a stranger to my brothers,
an alien to my own mother's sons."
(Psalm 69:8)**

WHAT IS the Root Cause of Loneliness?

The suffering servant laments, longing for days past *"when my path was drenched with cream and the rock poured out for me streams of olive oil"* (Job 29:6). Prosperity, prestige, peace, no longer flow into Job's life.

But he misses something else: the major lesson being reinforced through his trials—the privilege of fellowship with the Lord God Almighty. Wrongly believing that God has abandoned him, Job reminisces about when *"God's intimate friendship blessed my house"* (Job 29:4), and it turns out that the traumatic testing and the seeming absence of God has taken a toll.

Job indeed may be blameless, exhibiting a life characterized by obedience, but he certainly isn't *sinless*.

Pride and rebellion surface as Job's vehemence in defending his integrity soon malign and misrepresent God, prompting a sharp rebuke from God Himself.

"Will the one who contends with the Almighty correct him? Let him who accuses God answer him! ... Would you discredit my justice? Would you condemn me to justify yourself?" (Job 40:2, 8)

Job's story ends with the man of God humbled, repentant, and doubly restored of all he had lost. Job never curses God, yet divine correction still needs to be dispensed. And with that comes a renewed understanding of the importance of submitting to the sovereignty of God, as well as a greater awareness that God's faithful presence and fellowship are Job's greatest blessings of all, even when he doesn't understand or like what's going on in his life.

Your longing to belong is natural because God has placed within each of us a basic need for relationship with Him and with others. Don't seek to dull the pain of loneliness by finding substitutes to fill the void. Seeking comfort in food, shopping, alcohol, illegal drugs, or sexual encounters may offer fleeting pleasure, but these will cause you emotional or physical harm in the long run. Instead of focusing on your personal need, refocus on your relationship with Christ, leaning on His understanding and drawing from His strength.

"I have set the LORD always before me.
Because he is at my right hand,
I will not be shaken."
(Psalm 16:8)

▶ Wrong Belief:

"I must have the love and acceptance of others to feel significant and to fulfill my need to belong."

"You have taken from me my closest friends and have made me repulsive to them. I am confined and cannot escape." (Psalm 88:8)

▶ Right Belief:

"I want to have meaningful relationships with others, but I must first cultivate real intimacy with the Lord, who is always with me and will never leave me. Only out of a secure relationship with Him can I courageously move toward others in love regardless of their responses toward me."

"Where can I go from your Spirit? Where can I flee from your presence? If I go up to the heavens, you are there; if I make my bed in the depths, you are there. If I rise on the wings of the dawn, if I settle on the far side of the sea, even there your hand will guide me, your right hand will hold me fast." (Psalm 139:7–10)

God's Plan of Salvation for You

FOUR POINTS OF GOD'S PLAN

#1 God's Purpose for You is *Salvation*.

What was God's motivation in sending Christ to earth?

To express His love for you by saving you! The Bible says ...

"For God so loved the world that he gave his one and only Son, that whoever believes in him shall not perish but have eternal life. For God did not send his Son into the world to condemn the world, but to save the world through him." (John 3:16–17)

What was Jesus' purpose in coming to earth?

To forgive your sins, to empower you to have victory over sin, and to enable you to live a fulfilled life! Jesus said ...

"I have come that they may have life, and that they may have it more abundantly." (John 10:10 NKJV)

#2 Your Problem is *Sin*.

What exactly is sin?

Sin is living independently of God's standard—knowing what is right, but choosing what is wrong. The Bible says ...

"Anyone, then, who knows the good he ought to do and doesn't do it, sins." (James 4:17)

What is the major consequence of sin?

Spiritual "death," eternal separation from God. Scripture states ...

"Your iniquities [sins] have separated you from your God. ... The wages of sin is death, but the gift of God is eternal life in Christ Jesus our Lord." (Isaiah 59:2; Romans 6:23)

#3 God's Provision for You is the *Savior*.

Can anything remove the penalty for sin?

Yes! Jesus died on the cross to personally pay the penalty for your sins. The Bible says ...

"God demonstrates his own love for us in this: While we were still sinners, Christ died for us." (Romans 5:8)

What is the solution to being separated from God?

Believe in (entrust your life to) Jesus Christ as the only way to God the Father.

Jesus says ...

"I am the way and the truth and the life. No one comes to the Father except through me. ... Believe in the Lord Jesus, and you will be saved." (John 14:6; Acts 16:31)

#4 Your Part is *Surrender*.

Give Christ control of your life, entrusting yourself to Him.

"Jesus said to his disciples, 'If anyone would come after me, he must deny himself and take up his cross and follow me. For whoever wants to save his life will lose it, but whoever loses his life for me will find it. What good will it be for a man if he gains the whole world, yet forfeits his soul? Or what can a man give in exchange for his soul?'" (Matthew 16:24–26)

Place your faith in (rely on) Jesus Christ as your personal Lord and Savior and reject your "good works" as a means of earning God's approval.

"It is by grace you have been saved, through faith—and this not from yourselves, it is the gift of God—not by works, so that no one can boast." (Ephesians 2:8–9)

The moment you choose to receive Jesus as your Lord and Savior—entrusting your life to Him—He comes to live inside you. Then He gives you His power to live the fulfilled life God has planned for you.

If you want to be fully forgiven by God and become the person God created you to be, you can tell Him in a simple, heartfelt prayer like this:

PRAYER OF SALVATION

God, I want a real relationship with You.
I admit that many times I've failed
to go Your way and instead
chosen to go my own way.
Please forgive me for my sins.
Jesus, thank You for dying on the cross
to pay the penalty for my sins
and for rising from the dead to provide new
life. Come into my life to be my Lord and
my Savior. Place Your hope in my heart
and teach me to put my confidence in You.
Make me the person You created me to be.
In Your holy name I pray. Amen.

What Can You Expect Now?

If you sincerely prayed this prayer, look what God says!

> **"Never will I leave you; never will I forsake you." (Hebrews 13:5)**

If you sincerely prayed this prayer, look what God says about you!

> **"Therefore, if anyone is in Christ, he is a new creation; the old has gone, the new has come! All this is from God, who reconciled us to himself through Christ and gave us the ministry of reconciliation." (2 Corinthians 5:17–18)**

STEPS TO SOLUTION

She is a widow who refuses to languish in loneliness. Ruth's remedy isn't hastily remarrying or surrounding herself with as many people as possible. It's in reaching out and building a bridge—to her embittered and widowed mother-in-law—that Ruth finds purpose, fulfillment, companionship, and ultimately *reward*.

Naomi loses her husband and two sons while living in the land of Moab, escaping a lengthy famine in Judah. She urges her two daughters-in-law to return to their homes because, now that food is plentiful, Naomi has decided to go back to her homeland. Both Ruth and Orpah are reluctant to part from Naomi. Love and loss undeniably link the three women together, but the cord of compassion can't—*won't*—be cut by Ruth.

Feeling stuck in a state of loneliness is like living without eyes and ears. You are unable to see the loving potential in those around you—those who may be "suitable helpers" and those who may also be searching for a friend. Likewise, you are deaf to the messages of hope and encouragement surrounding you—in your place of worship, in the Bible, and on the lips of friends and loved ones. Through placing your trust in God, you have the power of God available to you to fully see and hear, to move past your barriers of fear and doubt, and to build a bridge of connection to your brothers and sisters in Christ.

"We proclaim to you what we have seen and heard, so that you also may have fellowship with us. And our fellowship is with the Father and with his Son, Jesus Christ."
(1 John 1:3)

When you feel as if the entire world has abandoned you, as if no one understands your pain and sorrow, the Bible promises that the Lord is with you and He will never leave you.

KEY VERSE TO MEMORIZE

"The LORD himself goes before you and will be with you; he will never leave you nor forsake you. Do not be afraid; do not be discouraged."
(Deuteronomy 31:8)

Key Passage to Read

Psalm 63:1–8

In your loneliness and despair, have you distanced yourself from the Lord?

It is never too late to draw near to Him again. You are His precious child. And when you do return to Him, you will be welcomed with open arms.

This Scripture reflects the heartfelt joy of the psalmist when returning home to the shelter of God's unconditional love and acceptance.

"O God, you are my God,
earnestly I seek you; my soul thirsts for you,
my body longs for you, in a dry and weary
land where there is no water.
I have seen you in the sanctuary
and beheld your power and your glory.
Because your love is better than life,
my lips will glorify you. I will praise you as
long as I live, and in your name I will lift up
my hands. My soul will be satisfied as with
the richest of foods; with singing lips my
mouth will praise you.
On my bed I remember you;
I think of you through the watches of the
night. Because you are my help,
I sing in the shadow of your wings.
My soul clings to you;
your right hand upholds me."
(Psalm 63:1–8)

In these eight verses, David declares ...

▶ **His relationship** with God (v. 1)

▶ **His pursuit** of God (v. 1)

▶ **His need** of God (v. 1)

▶ **His past experience** of God (v. 2)

▶ **His evaluation** of God's love (v. 2)

▶ **His response** to God's love (vv. 3–6)

▶ **His reliance** on God (v. 7)

▶ **His response** to God's help (vv. 7–8)

▶ **His acknowledgment** of God's support (v. 8)

Orpah ultimately returns to *"her people and her gods"* (Ruth 1:15), but Ruth delivers perhaps the most beautiful discourse on commitment in all of Scripture and doggedly determines that Naomi's God will be her God as well.

> **"Don't urge me to leave you
> or to turn back from you. Where you go I
> will go, and where you stay I will stay. Your
> people will be my people and your God my
> God. Where you die I will die, and there I
> will be buried. May the Lord deal with me,
> be it ever so severely, if anything but death
> separates you and me."**
> **(Ruth 1:16–17)**

And so Ruth begins to serve, going into fields and gleaning behind harvesters, picking up leftover grain to provide for Naomi. By the providence of God, Ruth winds up gleaning in a field owned by a man named Boaz, who is a close relative of Naomi. He is a gracious, well-respected man who protects and abundantly provides for Ruth.

Boaz will become an even greater blessing to both women, as God's perfect provision for their loneliness and need. Even as you learn to walk with the Lord as your constant companion, there will be times of loneliness. The following questions and answers may help you when you are lonely.

As you seek to know what your loneliness looks like, answer the following questions.[30]

Do you struggle with feelings of loneliness? ___

_____

When do you feel the loneliest? _____

_____

_____

What are your thoughts when you feel lonely? _

_____

_____

_____

When was the first time you remember feeling lonely? _____

_____

Do you blame yourself for your loneliness? ___

_____

Do you blame others for your loneliness? ____

_____

Have you talked to God about your loneliness?

_____

Have you talked with a friend about your loneliness? _____

_____

Do you think no one understands your feelings of loneliness? _____

_____

What have you done in the past to alleviate your loneliness? _____

_____

_____

Could you try something similar to change your present loneliness? _____

_____

Does your loneliness ever go away completely?

_____

_____

What does a typical day look like for you? ____

_____

_____

_____

_____

What are your outside activities? _____

_____

_____

_____

What are your interests and hobbies? _____

_____

_____

_____

**"Surely you desire truth in the inner parts;
you teach me wisdom in the inmost place."
(Psalm 51:6)**

Learning to take charge of your thinking is critically important for one simple reason: Your thoughts exert a powerful influence on your emotions, and together, your thoughts and feelings direct your actions. When the language center of your brain is focused on truthful statements, this positive focus can override your painful negative feelings. In this way, your thoughts determine your emotions.

Think of your thoughts as a symphony conductor and your emotions as an orchestra. As such, your thoughts produce and "conduct" your feelings. When you are *feeling* lonely and sad, evaluate your *thoughts*, and you will find that they correspond to your emotions. When you change your thoughts, you may find your feelings lining up with what you are thinking.

Therefore, the next time you are in the throes of loneliness—with your emotions spiraling downward—empower the language center of your brain by thinking and saying positive comments, and you will diminish the power of your negative feelings!

The Word of God is not silent on the importance of thinking. The apostle Paul said ....

> **"Finally, brothers, whatever is true, whatever is noble, whatever is right, whatever is pure, whatever is lovely, whatever is admirable— if anything is excellent or praiseworthy— think about such things."**
> **(Philippians 4:8)**

To equip you to control your thoughts ...

▶ **ANALYZE your thoughts** when you feel lonely.

- Realize negative situations contribute to lonely feelings. Ask yourself, "What am I *thinking* that is making me feel so lonely?"

- Remember your emotions react before the *problem-solving center* of your brain can accurately assess a negative situation. Say to yourself, "I need to breathe deeply, pray for wisdom, and give myself time to analyze what is going on inside of me."

- Use *words* to counter your feelings in order to lessen the strength of your painful emotions and take charge of them. Say to yourself, "These cruel words only reflect a wounded heart."

> **"There is a way that seems right to a man, but in the end it leads to death."**
> **(Proverbs 14:12)**

▶ USE **the language center of your brain** to evaluate your emotions.

- Ask yourself:

  "Why am I feeling this way?"

  "What lie(s) am I believing about myself?"

  "What wrong thoughts am I believing about others?"

- Evaluate the outcome of your painful situation.

  "Is it 'the end of the world'?" (No!)

  "What is the worst thing that could happen?"

  "Is God not powerful enough to get me through this?"

- Identify your losses of love, significance, and/or security (your three basic, God-given inner needs).[31]

  "Is my need for love not being met?"

  "Is my need for significance unmet?"

  "Is my need for security going unmet?"

> " ... take captive every thought
> to make it obedient to Christ."
> (2 Corinthians 10:5)

▶ ENGAGE **the problem-solving portion of your brain** to resolve your feelings of loneliness.

- Look for erroneous thinking, such as overestimating the severity of the present situation. Counter negative thoughts with positive ones. Repeat:

"I am not alone."

"I can handle anything with God's help."

- Curtail catastrophic thinking by emotionally detaching from the situation enough to make a truly objective appraisal of the *real* impact it is having on you and on your life.

"What exactly is happening?"

"What positive outcome could occur from this situation?"

"How might God use this for good in my life?"

- Determine to practice positive thinking to increase the odds of having a positive outcome. Ask yourself:

"What can I learn from this about myself? About God? About others?"

"How can I glorify God in this situation?"

"How can this situation help me grow in my dependence on the Lord?"

> **"I can do everything through him who gives me strength."**
> **(Philippians 4:13)**

▶ **EXPOSE your automatic, negative thoughts** that lead to excessive feelings of loneliness.

- If you feel undeserving of meaningful relationships, tell yourself, "I am loved by God, and He has created me for loving, meaningful relationships."

- If you belittle yourself by referring to yourself as "stupid, a loser, flawed, or defective," discard such degrading names and tell yourself truthfully, "I have received genuine compliments from others, and God has promised to be my sufficiency. I am a new creation in Christ and am being made perfect in Him."

- If you overgeneralize, you rob yourself of hope, assuming you will "always" be alone or "never" be happy. Drop "always" and "never" from your vocabulary, and celebrate your successes. Tell yourself:

  "God is in me and is faithfully working to accomplish His purposes through me. My joy is complete in Him."

  "I can have the loving relationship He designed for me."

  "I can achieve His purpose."

- If you live with a dialogue of demands—what you "should, must, have to, or ought to do"— begin thinking in terms of what you would "like, prefer, or wish for."

"I would appreciate being invited to the dinner, but if I'm not, it's not the end of the world."

"I would prefer to be liked by him, but if I'm not, I will live. After all, God has promised to meet my needs."

"I wish I would be accepted into that organization, but if I'm not, God still has something for me. That is in my best interest."

"I would love to be recognized for my contribution to the team, but God recognizes my accomplishments and is pleased with them."

"Do not conform any longer to the pattern of this world, but be transformed by the renewing of your mind."
(Romans 12:2)

▶ **DISARM your thoughts that produce loneliness** by asking yourself questions that produce valid, optimistic thoughts.

- If you isolate from others—thinking you will do something embarrassing—ask yourself:

"How fatal is embarrassment?"

"When was the last time I was embarrassed and what was the result?"

"Since everyone feels embarrassed from time to time, does it mean they are stupid or just normal like me?"

"Can't God help me overcome any embarrassing situation I might encounter?"

- If you assume that others think negatively about you, ask yourself:

"Have they done anything to confirm my suspicions?"

"If I don't think negatively about them, why would they think negatively about me? Could they be similarly concerned about what I think about them?"

"Why would they be thinking about me in the first place?"

"Isn't God the one I should be concerned about pleasing rather than people?"

- If you delay starting a new activity because of a fear of failing, ask yourself:

"Aren't my chances of succeeding better if I remain positive in my attitude and just take one step at a time?"

"Why am I giving in to fear by procrastinating?"

"Can't God and I successfully meet this challenge together?"

- If you think you are powerless and unable to cope with a negative situation and unpleasant outcome, ask yourself:

"What solid resources do I have in the form of supportive people, finances, health, talents, and skills to help me out?"

"What steps can I take to address the situation?"

"Hasn't God been faithful to help me through tough times in the past?"

"Can't I count on Him to be there for me now?"

**"Then you will know the truth,
and the truth will set you free."
(John 8:32)**

By dealing with the mental aspects of loneliness—practicing the skill of *controlling your thoughts*—you are laying a foundation necessary for removing the power of loneliness from your life.

The book of Lamentations emphasizes the impact of your thoughts, of what you say to yourself, and what you *call to mind:*

**"Yet this I call to mind and therefore I have hope: Because of the LORD's great love we are not consumed, for his compassions never fail. They are new every morning; great is your faithfulness.
I say to myself, 'The LORD is my portion; therefore I will wait for him.'"
(Lamentations 3:21–24)**

Isn't it interesting that not until God and Adam had an established relationship did God create Eve to be Adam's companion? In fact, there is no indication that Adam was even aware of his "aloneness" until he was naming the living creatures and realized there was no suitable mate for him (Genesis 2:19–22).

The implication is that we are created first for a relationship with God and second for a relationship with one another. Your bridge to God must be strong and sturdy, like a cable-stayed bridge replete with steel. Large, upright, steel supports and strong steel cables guarantee this bridge to weather the strongest storms. Other bridges around you may falter and crumble, but this one promises to stand firm, to faithfully function when you need it the most. If you reverse the order and make relationships with others your primary focus and God your secondary focus, you will have misplaced priorities and collapsing bridges.

Jesus said the greatest commandment is to love God and the second is to love others. Only as you find your security and stability in God will you be healthy enough to form secure and stable relationships with others. Your completeness must be found in Him. Otherwise, you will be looking for it in others but experiencing one frustrating relationship after another, looking to people for that which can be found only in God.

Before seeking to build bridges to others through personal relationships or through ministry relationships, first build a bridge to God. Jesus said, *"'Love the Lord your God with all your heart and with all your soul and with all your mind.' This is the first and greatest commandment. And the second is like it: 'Love your neighbor as yourself'"* (Matthew 22:37–39).

▶ Go to God's Word.

- Read your Bible on a daily basis, following a specific reading plan (for example, read through the four Gospels to learn the life of Jesus, or read one chapter in Proverbs and five Psalms each day– completing both books in one month).

- Identify verses or passages that seem especially poignant to you.

- Begin to memorize meaningful Bible verses by writing them on index cards and reading them throughout the day.

- Listen to scripturally sound Bible teachers on Christian radio or television.

- Look for ways to apply Scripture to your everyday life.

"Then they cried to the Lord in their trouble, and he saved them from their distress. He sent forth his word and healed them; he rescued them from the grave." (Psalm 107:19–20)

▶ **Expect God to do a new thing.**

- Begin to think about life from a biblical perspective.

- Leave your past way of living behind.

- Make a list of the new things God is doing in your life, new desires and interests you are acquiring.

- Give yourself time to adjust to the new life you have in Christ and the new creation He is making of you.

- Start a prayer journal, recording your prayers to God and the thoughts He impresses on your heart.

**"Forget the former things; do not dwell on the past. See, I am doing a new thing! Now it springs up; do you not perceive it? I am making a way in the desert and streams in the wasteland."
(Isaiah 43:18–19)**

▶ **Immerse yourself in inspirational music.**

- Listen to Christian radio in your car and at home.

- Pay close attention to the words you are hearing.

- Avoid listening to spiritually oppressive music.

- Choose your favorite inspirational music from various artists and styles.

- Sing songs containing Scripture as prayers to God.

> "My heart is steadfast,
> O God, my heart is steadfast;
> I will sing and make music."
> (Psalm 57:7)

▶ **Begin attending a group Bible study.**

- Find someone to lead a Bible study in your home if you don't feel comfortable leading one yourself.

- Join a small group Bible study with homework or specific assignments requiring you to study the Bible for yourself.

- Start a weekly group, encouraging one another in common areas of interest or concern.

- Share biblical encouragement for every problem.

- Do a Bible study on the computer with a group of friends or with just one person and hold each other accountable.

> "Let us not give up meeting together, as some are in the habit of doing, but let us encourage one another—and all the more as you see the Day approaching."
> (Hebrews 10:25)

▶ **Read about Christian role models.**

- Learn how other Christians (pastors, teachers, friends) handle adverse situations.

- Watch movies and/or documentaries on the lives of Christian leaders and other caring people.

- Study the life of Jesus Christ (the book of Matthew).

- Read about other role models in Scripture (the story of Joseph in Genesis chapters 37–50 or the book of Ruth).

- Read biographies about Christian role models (Corrie ten Boom, Jonathan Edwards).

"You became imitators of us and of the Lord; in spite of severe suffering, you welcomed the message with the joy given by the Holy Spirit. And so you became a model to all the believers in Macedonia and Achaia."
(1 Thessalonians 1:6–7)

One of the best antidotes for your loneliness is helping others, moving your focus from trying to meet your own needs to trying to help meet the needs of others. Like a beam bridge that generally covers short distances and is designed to resist bending, be up close and help sustain the weight of others' burdens. Ask God to help you not bend and break under the load, but to joyfully and faithfully support those He brings into your life in need of help and encouragement.

God designed relationships to be rewarding. He calls it the principle of "sowing and reaping." When you sow seeds of kindness and friendship in the lives of others, you will eventually reap the rewards of kindness and friendship in your own life. Just as the beam bridge is one of the simplest forms ever designed, remember simple acts of kindness can go a long way. A warm smile, a kind word, an invitation to lunch all communicate love and concern.

> **"Do not be deceived: God cannot be mocked. A man reaps what he sows."**
> **(Galatians 6:7)**

▶ **Understand the pain of others.**

- Imagine how you would feel in the same situation.

- Look for practical ways to help.

- Don't be critical.

- Know that it is by the grace of God that you are not in the same situation.

- Be a good listener.

"Recalling your tears, I long to see you, so that I may be filled with joy." (2 Timothy 1:4)

▶ **Look for ways to express love to others.**

- Offer help to someone in need (shop for groceries, prepare a meal, carpool, etc.).

- Send an encouraging card or note to someone.

- Help someone complete a task.

- Give someone a small gift (flowers, cookies, bookmark, etc.) communicating God's love.

- Perform random acts of kindness without expecting anything in return.

"Greater love has no one than this, that he lay down his life for his friends." (John 15:13)

▶ **Don't demand change.**

- Be flexible.

- Give others time to grow. Pray for them.

- Have a heart of love and acceptance for others.

- Make every attempt for peace.

- Don't require perfection from yourself or others.

> **"The wise in heart are called discerning,
> and pleasant words promote instruction."**
> **(Proverbs 16:21)**

▶ **Decide to diversify your activities and goals.**

- Give others the opportunity to know you.

- Be open to change.

- Participate in new and different activities.

- Be willing to give up old activities that are no longer useful or edifying.

- Pray for God's direction in choosing your activities.

> **"Sing to him a new song;
> play skillfully, and shout for joy."**
> **(Psalm 33:3)**

▶ **Initiate invitations (calls, visits).**

- Write letters to out-of-town friends and relatives.

- Invite people to have lunch or dinner with you.

- Invite people to your home.

- Offer your home for meetings and social gatherings.

- Join a committee in your church, welcoming visitors and new members.

- Initiate calls to people, asking them how they are doing.

"Then Jesus said to his host, 'When you give a luncheon or dinner, do not invite your friends, your brothers or relatives, or your rich neighbors; if you do, they may invite you back and so you will be repaid.
But when you give a banquet, invite the poor, the crippled, the lame, the blind, and you will be blessed. Although they cannot repay you, you will be repaid at the resurrection of the righteous.'"
(Luke 14:12–14)

▶ **Rid yourself of bitterness.**

- Pray for your enemies and those who have hurt you.

- Focus on the blessings in your life.

- Trust your choices to God. He is sovereign.

- Allow God to handle your hurts and disappointments.

- Bless others and leave vengeance to God.

- Forgive others and give them the same grace God gives you.

"See to it that no one misses the grace of God and that no bitter root grows up to cause trouble and defile many."
(Hebrews 12:15)

Ruth not only helps Naomi; she carefully heeds her advice. *"Wash ... perfume yourself ... put on your best clothes,"* Naomi instructs, and after Boaz has finished dinner and drifts off to sleep, *"Uncover his feet and lie down."* When he wakes up, *"He will tell you what to do. 'I will do whatever you say,'"* Ruth answered (Ruth 3:3–5).

Ruth is following the Jewish custom of the kinsman-redeemer, whereby the closest relative has the opportunity to marry a childless widow and raise children in her dead husband's name. When Boaz awakes and finds Ruth at his feet, followed by her statement, *"Spread the corner of your garment over me, since you are a kinsman-redeemer"* (Ruth 3:9), Boaz knows exactly what is going on. Ruth wants him to marry her.

Moved by the compassion and character of Ruth, Boaz indeed marries her and they bring forth a son, Obed, who is the grandfather of King David and *the delight of Naomi*. And Ruth is praised for all she has done to abate the loneliness and despair of her mother-in-law.

> **"For your daughter-in-law,**
> **who loves you and who is better**
> **to you than seven sons,**
> **has given him birth."**
> **(Ruth 4:15)**

God did not create us to live in isolation but to have fellowship with one another. Realize that your relationship with the Lord will also mean building a bridge to others. The Bible says ...

"For none of us lives to himself alone and none of us dies to himself alone."
(Romans 14:7)

Love begets love, therefore, look for others who are lonely or who have unmet needs. Ask God to show you how to build a bridge to connect with them, like an arch bridge where the load is transmitted from the deck of the bridge to the land on both sides. As you partner with God in ministry, you stand alongside Him as a strong source of support for those in need. Side by side, empowered by His strength, you become an "arch bridge" designed by God to bear the weight of the worries and trials of this world without collapsing.

"This is how we know what love is: Jesus Christ laid down his life for us. And we ought to lay down our lives for our brothers."
(1 John 3:16)

BRIDGE

Bᴇ ᴀᴡᴀʀᴇ of the ways you have been helped or wish you had been helped.

▶ List the physical, emotional, and spiritual needs you now have or have experienced in the past that required the help of another person (for example, rearranging furniture, sharing hurts, community worship).

▶ List the ways others have met those needs in your life.

**"Now to each one the manifestation
of the Spirit is given for the common good."
(1 Corinthians 12:7)**

RECOGNIZE the ways others presently need help that you could be called to give.

▶ Check with nursing homes, retirement centers, and/or local churches to find elderly or shut-in members who have physical, emotional, or spiritual needs.

▶ Check area Christian or service ministries to identify needs they have for volunteers.

**"If one falls down, his friend can help him
up. But pity the man who falls
and has no one to help him up!"
(Ecclesiastes 4:10)**

IDENTIFY ways to help meet some of the needs you have identified.

▶ Evaluate your personal strengths, spiritual gifts, and physical resources for meeting the needs of others.

▶ Evaluate practical ways you can use your abilities and resources to meet some of these needs.

**"In the church God has appointed ...
those able to help others."
(1 Corinthians 12:28)**

Dᴇᴠᴇʟᴏᴘ a plan for building your bridge of help to others in need.

▶ Ask God to identify and give you a caring heart for the specific person or group of people He wants to help through you.

▶ Ask permission from proper authorities (for example, church or ministry leadership) or from specific individuals to be of help to them.

"Carry each other's burdens, and in this way you will fulfill the law of Christ." (Galatians 6:2)

Gᴇᴛ ɪɴᴠᴏʟᴠᴇᴅ with the people you plan to help.

▶ Spend time with the individual people and get to know each of them. Have a meal with them. Listen to their stories.

▶ Spend time identifying and strategizing with them the ways you can be of assistance to them.

"Let us not become weary in doing good, for at the proper time we will reap a harvest if we do not give up. Therefore, as we have opportunity, let us do good to all people, especially to those who belong to the family of believers." (Galatians 6:9–10)

EXTEND **help to those God has brought into your life.**

▶ Initiate calls, visits, and contacts, making all the arrangements necessary for providing the practical help you have committed to give.

▶ Initiate the initial provision of help and any ongoing help for the duration of time that such help is needed and/or for the time that you are able to provide it.

> **"Serve one another in love."**
> **(Galatians 5:13)**

HOW TO Overcome Loneliness

Since loneliness is common to all of us and can be effectively controlled, it is helpful to closely examine the elements of loneliness in your own life.

Knowledge alone cannot solve the problems loneliness causes, but knowledge coupled with wisdom can be very helpful in limiting the negative effects of loneliness in your life. While loneliness feels like an emotional problem based on unchangeable circumstances, it is actually a perception problem that can lead to emotional problems.

> **"For the LORD gives wisdom, and from his mouth come knowledge and understanding." (Proverbs 2:6)**

▶ Loneliness is having ...

- No one to talk to; to spend time with; to reach out and touch

- An empty lounge chair; a half empty bed; an emotionally empty heart

- A phone that never rings; mail that never comes; a doorbell that never chimes

- Time to spare, but no one with time to share

- A gift, but no one to give it to

- A house that is no longer a home

- A meal without fellowship

- A special occasion without a special person

- A car but not a passenger

- A new outfit, but nowhere to go and no one to wear it for

▶ Loneliness is overcome by ...

- Filling a once-empty table with dinner guests

- Not waiting for company but sending out invitations

- Making holidays festive by starting new traditions

- Calling others on the phone

- Mailing cards to family members and acquaintances

- Letting go of grudges and extending forgiveness

- Sharing a meal with a shut-in

- Giving gifts to needy children

- Finding someone to listen to

- Taking the time to visit those in need of company

"Then the righteous will answer him, 'Lord, when did we see you hungry and feed you, or thirsty and give you something to drink? When did we see you a stranger and invite you in, or needing clothes and clothe you? When did we see you sick or in prison and go to visit you?' The King will reply, 'I tell you the truth, whatever you did for one of the least of these brothers of mine, you did for me.'" (Matthew 25:37–40)

Expect a Period of Sadness

QUESTION: "What are the loneliest times I'll face now that my mate is gone?"

ANSWER: The most emotional times will be holidays, birthdays, and anniversaries. But loneliness and grief can come in waves when you least expect it, when you hear a song that was meaningful to you both, or when you see something reminding you of your beloved mate. Expect a period of sadness and grief. Mourning a significant loss is a healthy and natural part of life. It helps bring acceptance of your new reality, which in turn clears the path for you to eventually feel joy.

"[There is] a time to weep and a time to laugh, a time to mourn and a time to dance."
(Ecclesiastes 3:4)

We have all been rejected, and we all long to be accepted. But rather than focusing on fear of rejection, focus on reaching out to others regardless of differences.

Think about it: You respond positively when you find that others are interested in you. When someone genuinely wants to know more about you, doesn't that warm your heart? You can be like a closed rosebud blossoming into full bloom when you meet someone who sincerely reaches out to you, nurturing you—as with water and fertilizer—caring that you grow to your full potential.

If you want to reach out to others but don't know where to start, begin with ordinary questions. Your heartfelt interest will build a bridge to further communication. Gradually ease into the questions.

As you talk with someone you don't know well, you could say, "I've never heard you talk about your childhood. Where did you grow up? What was it like living there? What was the most character-building experience of your childhood?" The Bible poetically emphasizes well-spoken words:

"A word aptly spoken is like apples of gold in settings of silver."
(Proverbs 25:11)

Conversation Starters

The following questions can help you initiate conversations with others.

▶ **Questions about early family life:**

- Where were you born and raised? How did you feel about where you lived?

- What kind of work did your mom and dad do?

- What kind of relationship did you have with your father? Your mother?

- Did you have brothers and sisters? Were you emotionally close to them? Where are they now? What do they do? Are you involved in each other's lives?

- Was there an activity your family enjoyed together when you were growing up?

- What was it *really* like for you growing up?

- If you could change anything about your childhood, what would it be?

▶ **Questions about school:**

- Did you like being a student?

- What did you enjoy/not enjoy about school?

- What do you remember most about school when you were a child?

- Did you have a favorite teacher? What made that teacher special?

- What was your favorite subject in school? Least favorite? Why?

- What extracurricular activities did you enjoy?

- What is your most painful or embarrassing memory from your days in school?

▶ **Questions about growing up:**

- Who was your childhood hero? Why?

- What did you dream of doing when you grew up? Why?

- Did you have a best friend? Why were you so close?

- Who encouraged you the most in your childhood?

- What was the most significant event in your childhood?

- What was the most fearful time?

- What was something you really hated doing as a child?

- What was your first job?

▶ **Questions about life today:**

- If you could have any job in the world, what would it be?

- What do you especially enjoy doing in your free time?

- What would be your ideal vacation?

- What skill or talent do you wish you had?

- Who is investing time, concern, and energy into your life right now? How?

- What do you like most about your life today?

- If you could change anything about yourself, what would it be?

▶ **Questions about spiritual life:**

- Do you think God has a purpose for your life?

- How would you describe God?

- Did you attend a church growing up? What was it like?

- Did anything significant occur in your spiritual life when you were young?

- What is the most meaningful experience you've had in your spiritual life?

- If you could come into a true relationship with Jesus Christ, would you want to?

- What do you think God wants you to do that you haven't done yet?

Pray that you will be able to ask the right questions at the right time. When you do, you will be amazed at the difference in your relationships with others.

"The purposes of a man's heart are deep waters, but a man of understanding draws them out." (Proverbs 20:5)

Making It through the Holidays

QUESTION: "How can I make it through the holidays?"

ANSWER: First, commit to rejoice in the blessing of having sweet memories. Then, make plans to be with others on sentimental, special days.

▶ Be with comforting family or friends.

▶ Reach out to someone in need.

> "Two are better than one,
> because they have a good return
> for their work: If one falls down,
> his friend can help him up.
> But pity the man who falls
> and has no one to help him up!"
> (Ecclesiastes 4:9–10)

Learn to lean on the Lord in your loneliness. He can and will comfort you. Allow Him to meet your deepest longings and fill you with His love. You do this through prayer and searching for Him in Scripture.

Pray, thanking Him for being the God of all comfort.

Thank you, God, that you COMFORT.

CARE for me with compassion

"Because of the LORD's great love we are not consumed, for his compassions never fail." (Lamentations 3:22)

OFFER strength when I am weak

"I can do everything through him who gives me strength." (Philippians 4:13)

MEET all of my needs

"And my God will meet all your needs according to his glorious riches in Christ Jesus." (Philippians 4:19)

FORGIVE and forget my sins

"For I will forgive their wickedness and will remember their sins no more." (Hebrews 8:12)

Offer hope for the future

"'I know the plans I have for you,' declares the LORD, 'plans to prosper you and not to harm you, plans to give you hope and a future.'" (Jeremiah 29:11)

Reassure me of Your love

"I have loved you with an everlasting love; I have drawn you with loving-kindness." (Jeremiah 31:3)

Turn my pain into joy

"Weeping may remain for a night, but rejoicing comes in the morning." (Psalm 30:5)

God has not created you and set you adrift in a sea of loneliness. He not only knows the intimate details of your life. He has your best interests foremost in His mind. He is, *"the Father of compassion and the God of all comfort."* (2 Corinthians 1:3)

ALONE BUT NOT LONELY

You may feel lonely, but you are never alone! Take comfort in God's promise that, no matter the circumstances, you are never alone.

—June Hunt

SCRIPTURES TO MEMORIZE

Can we be **all alone** but **not** feel **alone**?

*"[Jesus said] ... You will leave me **all alone**. Yet I am **not alone**, for my Father is with me."* (John 16:32)

How do you handle the **fear** that no one will be **with you** to **help you**?

*"Do not **fear**, for I am **with you**; do not be dismayed, for I am your God. I will strengthen you and **help you**; I will uphold you with my righteous right hand."* (Isaiah 41:10)

How does **God** use **families** to help those who are **lonely**?

*"**God** sets the **lonely** in **families**."* (Psalm 68:6)

Should I **look not only** to my **own interests** but **also** to **the interests of others**?

*"Each of you should **look not only** to your **own interests**, but **also** to **the interests of others**."* (Philippians 2:4)

Why is it important to pray for a **friend** who **can help** you **up**?

*"If one falls down, his **friend can help** him **up**. But pity the man who falls and has no **one** to help him up!"* (Ecclesiastes 4:10)

What if we aren't **in the habit** of **meeting together** with other people?

> *"Let us not give up **meeting together**, as some are **in the habit** of doing, but let us encourage one another—and all the more as you see the Day approaching."* (Hebrews 10:25)

Where can I **find rest** and **hope** for **my soul**?

> *"**Find rest**, O **my soul**, in God alone; my **hope** comes from him. He alone is my rock and my salvation; he is my fortress, I will not be shaken."* (Psalm 62:5–6)

Has **God** promised to **never leave** me **nor forsake** me?

> *"The **LORD** himself goes before you and will be with you; he will **never leave** you **nor forsake** you. Do not be afraid; do not be discouraged."* (Deuteronomy 31:8)

How can I **forget the former things** that caused me such pain in the **past**?

> *"**Forget the former things**; do not dwell on the **past**. See, I am doing a new thing! ... I am making a way in the desert and streams in the wasteland."* (Isaiah 43:18–19)

I don't want to keep **crying**— will my **tears** last forever?

> *"He will wipe every **tear** from their eyes. There will be no more death or mourning or **crying** or pain, for the old order of things has passed away."* (Revelation 21:4)

NOTES

1. John Haggai, *How to Win Over Loneliness* (Eugene, OR: Harvest House, 1988), 20.

2. *Merriam-Webster Collegiate Dictionary*, s.v. "Lonely," http://www.m-w.com; Don Baker, *Lord, I've Got a Problem* (Eugene, OR: Harvest House, 1988), 13.

3. *Merriam-Webster Collegiate Dictionary*, s.v. "Lonely."

4. Wilhelm Gesenius and Samuel Prideaux Tregelles, *Gesenius' Hebrew and Chaldee Lexicon to the Old Testament Scriptures* (Bellingham, WA: Logos Research Systems, Inc, 2003), 345.

5. James Swanson, *Dictionary of Biblical Languages With Semantic Domains: Greek (New Testament)*, electronic ed. (Oak Harbor: Logos Research Systems, Inc., 1997), #3670.

6. Tim Clinton and Ron Hawkins, *The Quick Reference Guide to Biblical Counseling* (Grand Rapids: Baker, 2009), 151.

7. Clinton and Hawkins, *The Quick Reference Guide to Biblical Counseling*, 151.

8. Clinton and Hawkins, *The Quick Reference Guide to Biblical Counseling*, 151.

9. *Merriam-Webster Collegiate Dictionary*, s.v. "Alone."

10. Swanson, *Dictionary of Biblical Languages With Semantic Domains: Greek (New Testament)*, electronic ed., #3668.

11. Swanson, *Dictionary of Biblical Languages With Semantic Domains: Greek (New Testament)*, electronic ed., #963.

12. Warren W. Weirsbe, *Lonely People: Biblical Lessons on Understanding and Overcoming Loneliness* (Grand Rapids: Baker, 2002), 11–12.

13. *Merriam-Webster Collegiate Dictionary*, s.v. "Solitude."

14. Tom Varney, *Loneliness*, (Colorado Springs: NavPress, 1992), 16.

15. Varney, *Loneliness*, 16.

16. Varney, *Loneliness*, 16.

17. Paul Tillich as quoted in Mike Nappa, *The Courage to Be Christian: Entering a Life of Spiritual Passion* (West Monroe, LA: Howard Publishing, 2001), 137.

18. J. Oswald Sanders, *Facing Loneliness: The Starting Point of a New Journey* (Grand Rapids: Discovery House, 1990), 23–24.

19. Sanders, *Facing Loneliness*, 24.

20. For this section see Sanders, *Facing Loneliness*, 23–25.

21. Wiersbe, *Lonely People*, 11.

22. Wiersbe, *Lonely People*, 11.

23. See Wiersbe, *Lonely People*, 11.

24. For this section see Haggai, *How to Win Over Loneliness*, 35.

25. Stephen S. Ivy, *The Promise and Pain of Loneliness* (Nashville: Broadman Press, 1989), 19.

26. Gary R Collins, Ph.D., *Christian Counseling—A Comprehensive Guide,* Dallas: Word Publishing, 1988, pp 94–98

27. Kerby Anderson, "Loneliness," Leadership U. (Plano, TX: Faculty Commons, 1993), http://www.leaderu.com/orgs/probe/docs/lonely.html.

28. Kerby Anderson, "Loneliness," Leadership U.

29. Kerby Anderson, "Loneliness," Leadership U.

30. Tim Clinton and Ron Hawkins, *The Quick Reference Guide to Biblical Counseling*, 151–152, 158.

31. Lawrence J. Crabb, Jr., *Understanding People: Deep Longings for Relationship*, Ministry Resources Library (Grand Rapids: Zondervan, 1987), 15–16; Robert S. McGee, *The Search for Significance*, 2nd ed. (Houston, TX: Rapha, 1990), 27–30.

SELECTED BIBLIOGRAPHY

Baker, Don. *Lord, I've Got a Problem*. Eugene, OR: Harvest House, 1988.

Carter, Leslie W., Paul D. Meier, and Frank B. Minirth. *Overcoming Loneliness*. Grand Rapids: Spire, 2000.

Elliot, Elisabeth. *Loneliness*. Nashville: Oliver-Nelson, 1988.

Haggai, John. *How to Win Over Loneliness*. Eugene, OR: Harvest House, 1988.

Hunt, June. *Bonding with Your Teen through Boundaries*. Wheaton, ILL: Crossway Books, 2010.

Hunt, June. *Caring for a Loved One with Cancer*. Wheaton, IL: Crossway Books, 2011.

Hunt, June. *Counseling Through Your Bible Handbook*. Eugene, Oregon: Harvest House Publishers, 2008.

Hunt, June. *Hope for Your Heart: Finding Strength in Life's Storms*. Wheaton, IL: Crossway Books, 2011.

Hunt, June. *How to Defeat Harmful Habits*. Eugene, OR: Harvest House, 2011.

Hunt, June. *How to Forgive ... When You Don't Feel Like It*. Eugene, Oregon: Harvest House Publishers, 2007.

Hunt, June. *How to Handle Your Emotions*. Eugene, Oregon: Harvest House Publishers, 2008.

Hunt, June. *How to Rise Above Abuse.* Eugene, OR: Harvest House, 2010.

Hunt, June. *Keeping Your Cool ... When Your Anger Is Hot!* Eugene, Oregon: Harvest House Publishers, 2009.

Hunt, June. *Seeing Yourself Through God's Eyes.* Eugene, Oregon: Harvest House Publishers, 2008.

Ivy, Steven S. *The Promise and Pain of Loneliness.* Nashville: Broadman, 1989.

Jeremiah, David. *Overcoming Loneliness.* Rev. ed. Nashville: Thomas Nelson, 1991.

"Loneliness" (self-help brochure) published by Counseling Center at the University of Illinois, found online at URL: http://www.counselingcenter.illinois.edu/?page_id=188

Mains, Karen Burton. *Lonely No More: A Woman's Journey to Personal, Marital, and Spiritual Healing.* Dallas: Word, 1993.

Sanders, J. Oswald. *Facing Loneliness: The Starting Point of a New Journey.* Grand Rapids: Discovery House, 1990.

Wiersbe, Warren W. *Lonely People: Biblical Lessons on Understanding and Overcoming Loneliness.* Living Lessons from God's Word. Grand Rapids: Baker, 2002.

June Hunt's HOPE FOR THE HEART minibooks are biblically-based, and full of practical advice that is relevant, spiritually-fulfilling and wholesome.

HOPE FOR THE HEART TITLES

www.hendricksonrose.com

The HOPE FOR THE HEART Biblical Counseling Library is Your Solution!

- Easy-to-read, perfect for anyone.
- Short. Only 96 pages. Good for the busy person.
- Christ-centered biblical advice and practical help
- Tested and proven over 20 years of June Hunt's radio ministry
- 30 titles in the series – each tackling a key issue people face today.
- Affordable. You or your church can give away, lend, or sell them.

Display available for churches and ministries.

www.hendricksonrose.com